KVASS

Copyright © 2012 Dan Woodske

Volume 1

About the Author

Dan Woodske lives in Beaver Falls Pennsylvania with his wife Kimberly and his best friend Bemus, who happens to be a 6 year-old gray and black stripped male cat.

He owns the Beaver Brewing Company™, an artesian nano-brewery in Beaver Falls, Pennsylvania which he shamelessly will self-promote right here, go to www.beaverbrewingcompany.com and drink our beer!

He is a graduate of the University of Pittsburgh and earned a degree in marketing...somehow that transferred into a beer business....

He has worked in politics, sales, marketing, as a maid, and also as a janitor. Not in that order...and yes, maid is correct.

Dan also has another book: *A Brewers Guide to Opening a Nanobrewery: Your $10,000 Brewery Consultant for $15.*

Furthermore he has a documentary *Beaver Falls: Where is Joe Namath?*

As you can see his interests are all over the place. Feel free to email him at dan@beaverbrewingcompany.com

A Note from the author...

My interest in Kvass began when I started the Beaver Brewing Company, a nano-brewery in Beaver Falls. The brewery focuses on "strange" off the wall beer styles and with some research I found there was a style of beer most Americans have never tasted, let alone heard of...that was Kvass.

I was really intrigued when I found out that this was a large part of Eastern European culture considering almost all of my ancestry is from that region.

I found out early on at my brewery that people really have a thirst for tastes that they are not familiar with. After the success of the kvass I started with a Roggenbier, another rare beer style. Then wet-hopped beers, then one with fresh basil, one with Nelson Sauvin Hops...and so on.

But I kept coming back to the kvass, and so did my customers. They really enjoyed it and soon some started bringing me in their OWN kvass they made at home.

Wanting to learn more about this unique ale I found that info (if any) was sparse, and often didn't provide enough detail to really give a clear picture of what Kvass was, why it has been so popular for over 1,000 years, and how it came about.

3

Even worse there was no book (at least none in English) out there that focused on the history of kvass...and good luck finding a recipe! Almost every recipe I found was a rehashing of the exact same one over and over and over...

After over a year of research (and brewing the drink almost non-stop) I compiled everything I learned from the brewing process.

From the health aspects of it, to the actual taste of the drinks, I tried to get everything I have found into this one small book. I mean it's good to have a healthy drink, but if it tastes good we are really in business!

More than learning about Kvass, I really want you to make this stuff. I have over 25 recipes in here, and I am sure at least a few of them will catch your eye and get your ass out of your recliner and into your kitchen. Either way, enjoy the journey and cheers to Kvass!

What is Kvass?

A very simple question with a very complex answer. First let's look at the Merriam-Webster® Dictionary definition: *a slightly alcoholic beverage of eastern Europe made from fermented mixed cereals and often flavored.*[1] Fairly straight forward, but open to a WIDE interpretation. What cereals? What Flavorings?

This is exactly what makes Kvass such an interesting drink, you can do almost whatever you want to it and tailor your recipe to fit your tastes...like it sour? You can do that....How about sweet? That can also be arranged.

While some Americans (including the writer of this book), consider it a beer, it really is in a class all by itself. The Brewers Association ® does not even have a classification of it in their Beer style guidelines as of 2012.

Some Kvass has bread included, some have fruit, many have lemons, honey is a common ingredient. So how do you know when you are drinking or making Kvass? I think the honorable Supreme Court Justice Potter Stewart summed up these hard to explain ideas with the phrase "I know it when I see it," to describe the

---

[1] http://www.merriam-webster.com/dictionary/kvass (3/13/2012)

threshold of pornography in the *Jacobellis vs. Ohio case of 1964*.[2]

Another characteristic that makes a traditional kvass a traditional kvass is the low amount of alcohol. Some brewers will make special kvass brews of the drink here or there but to store it for longer periods they will raise the alcohol anywhere from 3%-5% ABV (alcohol by volume)...traditional kvass is .5% - 2% ABV.

While it is still made with bread (usually) it isn't anything near what was made 1,000 years ago.

Usually Kvass is marked clearly when buying it commercially so you won't be surprised there. But what are the qualities of Kvass? Here are some things that are in all Kvass types:

1. It is a fermented drink.
2. Fermentable sugars will be present.
3. Water must be included.

After that it's wide open but here are some items that are in ALMOST all kvass styles.

1. Bread is almost always involved (or grains that make bread)

---

[2] http://en.wikipedia.org/wiki/I_know_it_when_I_see_it (1964 Jacobellis vs. Ohio)

2. Some sort of fruit (or sweetener) is included.
3. Usually a fairly cloudy drink when made at home.
4. The drink can be carbonated, but the majority of homemade Kvass (and almost 100% of the traditional kvass) is "flat".

As the saying goes "There is more than one way to skin a cat," there is absolutely more than one way to make kvass...or even describe it.

History of Kvass

Since you are reading this book you have surely heard of kvass at some point in your life but may have no idea that the first mention of Kvass was in about 1,000 A.D. That's correct, 1,000 A.D. While I am sure you all have read *The Primary Chronicle* (Russian: *Повесть временных лет*) which is sometimes translated into English as *Tale of the Bygone Years* I will bore you with some of the details of what the book was, and why it was important to the history of this ancient ale.

The Primary Chronicle was the history of the Kievan Rus'. This was a society / government of people that was founded by Prince Oleg in the late 800's. They lasted longer than many dynasties / governments of the time, but ceased to exist when the Mongol's got a taste for imperialism and overtook their territory in the 1,200's.

This chronicle was rumored to be written by a monk whose name was Nestor. In this book we find the first reference of Kvass. Actually it is mentioned several times in the book but it is mentioned in context of how it should be distributed by Prince Vladimir in 996 AD. [3]

3

Glants, Musya & Toomre, Joyce ed Food in Russian History and Culture 1997 Indiana University Press, Indianapolis Indiana.

He states to *"give food, honey, and Kvass to the people in Barrels"*. This wasn't just for the fun of it, he was getting baptized as a Christian and they were adopting Christianity as the official religion. Not something to scoff at for the time and it was to be met with celebration.

Kvass was so important that the Prince of an entire civilization was making sure that people were getting it so they could take part in the celebration.

Over the next few hundred years this became *THE* drink for peasants (as well as royalty) in Russia. It was not strange for cultures during these times to make something with their water.

Most inventions are out of necessity...not for fun. You may or may not know that the disposable diaper wasn't made for convenience; it was really made for the astronauts by NASA. Imagine going to the bathroom at zero gravity....Now that you have that picture of "stuff" floating around let's move onto more pleasant items...they NEEDED the disposable diaper and Russians NEEDED Kvass.

This "invention" was really a way to cleanse the water.

Kvass wasn't like today's beer that is usually enjoyed after work or at an afternoon BBQ, this was to be drunk for breakfast, lunch, and dinner.

This was the most common non-alcolic drink during the times that Peter the Great was ruling over Russia. Many even think that is was consumed more than water.[4]

While people sure were drinking a lot of kvass, you won't find the first written recipe for another 500+ years. Now I'm sure you have read the *Domostroi*, but if you haven't I will enlighten you...It is a Russian "how to" book for households. It is chalked full of information on cooking, manners, and how to take care of your family.

You can find an English translated version called *Domostroi: Rules for Russian Households in the Time of Ivan the Terrible*. In it you will find the first mention of an actual kvass recipe, *"Take four parts honey and strain it until it is clear. Put it in a jar and ferment it using an ordinary soft loaf, without additional yeast. When it is done, pour it into a cask."*[5]

In the recipe section you will find that recipe hasn't changed much over the last 500 or so years.

There is a group of people out there, you know them, the beer or wine "snob"...these are the people that

[4] http://www.tititudorancea.org/z/kvass.htm
[5] Pouncy, Carolyn Johnston translated, edition *The Domostroi, Rules for Russians Housholds in the time of Ivan the Terrible* Cornell University Press, Ithaca, NY 1994

literally turn up their nose when you order an "insufficient" beer at your local tavern or request the wrong year of cabernet at your favorite restaurant. There are also Kvass snobs out there…

This started around 1,400 A.D. when Prince Yuri wanted a Monastery in Zvenigorod. Soon after its final construction the monks there began brewing some of the best Kvass in the world. For the next 600+ years they continued to make it in their basement.

It is widely considered as some of the world's best traditionally made kvass.

But unless you decided to give your life to the church or make a quick visit there, you would never have it. That all changed in 2001 when they decided to sell to the public.

They stick to the traditional kvass…no preservatives at all and they toss it after 5 days. The monks say it is "живой" which translates into English as "Alive". These guys are serious…

Back to them being snobs…Father Ignaty who works at the church was once quoted saying that *"It is not profitable for them (large kvass makers) to make "live" kvass, so they are forced to poison people."*[6]

The monks still are making the kvass today and store it in large refrigerated tanks in their basement.

To illustrate just how important Kvass is in modern day Russian culture take a look at this story which I am sure received very little coverage at the time. During the Cold War *The Spokesman-Review* published an article by Robert C. Toth in 1976 detailing a venture the Communists took up in 1969 when the Russians bought a western canning line and were intent on getting more kvass out to the masses.

"The fiasco began in 1969, when the Russians bought a beer production line for the pasteurized canning of Kvass, previously bottled....The engineers quickly "divined," however, as Izvestia said, that the line was 'incomplete.' That's an understatement. Still needed were; Automated equipment...a rinsing unit, a unit to prepare the kvass, equipment to sort out rejects, a sterilizer, an elevator...",[7] and the list continues...Long story short they ended up buying the rest of equipment

6

http://www.sptimes.ru/index.php?action_id=2&story_id=265 10 – St. Petersburg Times (Issue #1389) Published July 11th 2008.
[7] *The Spokesman Review* – October 10th 1976 - page B17 – by Robert C. Toth – 94th year issue no. 149

that was needed and in 1971 were ready to give this the shot that the drink deserved.

Toth writes, *"It produced 7,128 cans of kvass, of which precisely 7,128 can were rejected."* The tin wasn't suitable for kvass and there wasn't even a pull tab on the cans, you had to use a nail to get the out the kvass!

While this is an interesting story what it really shows is just how important the drink is in Russian/Soviet history. The communists wasted 4 years of time, effort, and money just so they could get this drink out to their people. To fully understand this take into consideration the timing...We were in the middle of the space race and Russia was putting some of its' engineers "talents" into a kvass canning line.

It was even rarer for the Russians to admit they messed up on something that involved manufacturing. I mean for a country that stood behind "Workers of the World Unite" and controlled the media this was a rarity. But they had to let their people know they were trying to get good kvass out there and hit a snag.

While this history is interesting, I probably learned the most hands-on knowledge about Kvass from an ex-soviet, a really nice guy that popped into my brewery one day and ended up going home with 10 gallons of

Kvass! He grew up in the Communist Soviet Union where kvass was a very popular and tasty drink.

He said it was served in "hot dog like carts" all throughout the USSR. These vendors made traditional kvass with Bread, Lemons, and Raisins. He said as a child this was a staple and he loved the beverage (yes, kids drink kvass in Europe, they are not the prudes' we are here in America), but with the fall of communism also brought the fall of great kvass.

Here's a little history lesson…with communism profit didn't matter. Since the state owned everything there was little incentive to create economies of scale or scope. You could make kvass from the best (or most traditional) ingredients and sell it at cost. It didn't really matter because the Kremlin gave you everything you needed.

When communism fell people actually had to MAKE money and making great traditional kvass becomes expensive.

Compounding matters that this crazy capitalism brought (sarcasm being used here) is that when communism ceased to exist the government still enjoyed controlling people and some really crazy restrictions came down on street vendors. So bad were the regulations that in many of the countries where Kvass was popular kvass vendors were completely shut down

So in 1993 traditional kvass pretty much ceased to exist. He said they actually called it "93 Kvass" (maybe 1992 Kvass) in Lithuania if you could ever find a "real" kvass.

You're probably thinking, well the drink didn't disappear, I mean I did just buy a book about it...so what happened? For a few years it pretty much did disappear in the commercial market. Large commercial beverage companies began making kvass. And to make a profit they had to cut some corners.

One of the corners was eliminating the real bread, the real lemons, and the real sugar. Some even added preservatives to the drink which fudged with the taste.

Think of drinking fresh squeezed fruit juice then a concentrate "fruit juice" that contains 50% real juice. You can taste the difference...the same is true with Kvass.

The drink became commercialized and to fans of the recipe that had existed for over 1,000 years this didn't cut it.

He told me he hadn't even had Kvass in years since every one he has tried since his days growing up reminded him of "bad yeasty soda".

He made the 8-hour drive out to the brewery that Saturday to finally have traditional kvass and left happy.

I have consumed many commercialized Kvass drinks. Like anything some are much better than others and some are quite terrible. I would say almost none actually taste like homemade kvass. Some are close, but you can notice the difference.

I would highly recommend hunting down a bottle of this at your local Russian grocery store. If you don't have one locally, there are some sold online and found with relative ease.

Modern Day Kvass

So you want some kvass but your cooking skills consist of the microwave and canned soup. Do not fret, you can buy it commercially.

Make sure you read the label though. If it's not in Russian, it's probably not made with bread (or bread like extract) and it probably contains no yeast.

I have seen many "health" drinks out there labeled as Kvass but they contain no bread and are more like a fruit drink with lacto-fermentation and not traditional Kvass.

Like I said, stick to the Russian brands. There is one caveat to drinking many of the commercial brands; most taste nothing like or very little like homemade kvass.

Many serious kvass drinkers have told me they think it is a "yeasty soft drink" and I'd have to agree with the ones that I have tried. Some are very sugary with little to no bread taste.

There are several bakeries in the US that make kvass from their own bread and there are some excellent examples out there.

Check out the web to see if any are doing it near you. Most I have found are in Russian neighborhoods.

HOPEFULLY you bought this book for the recipes and not the historical perspective of kvass. While it's interesting to know how kvass came about, making it is much more rewarding.

It's fun to make your own then go out and buy the bottled stuff. I would do a taste test with your friends to see if they can tell.

The Health Aspects of Kvass

I call Kvass the "Russian Health Drink of the 10th Century" when I conduct Kvass tastings at the brewery.

People figured out pretty early in history that if you didn't get fruit you were going to get something else...scurvy. Since keeping your teeth has been popular for thousands of years adding fruit to Kvass just made sense.

Many traditional Kvass recipes added lemons to add vitamin C. In its first few hundred years it was thought that it could ward off disease such as cholera just by drinking this ale.

It's also healthier to drink than water...you may think that is arguable but consider this...how did most disease and sickness got passed around in biblical times up to through the 18th century? Quite often that disease came through the water supply. Again, this is something people picked up on quickly. Water is generally boiled (or heated) before the bread or flavoring is added.

Farmers that lived near ponds with stagnant water especially had to consider bacteria in their water. This is another reason that peasants found the drink so popular, not simply for taste, but survival.

Fermenting yeast also works as a sanitizer. Same goes for the alcohol. All of these aspects combined made

Kvass "healthier" to drink than water for the simple fact that it was actually "clean" and killed off much of the bacteria, viruses, and other bad stuff you may find in your water supply.

It is widely thought that Russians may have drunk more Kvass than water in areas where large amount of peasants lived.

These are the more ancient medicinal values to the drink, however with modern science we have figured out that these perceived values in kvass weren't all mystical, there was a whole lot of truth behind its healing power.

Fermented beverages kick up a lot of B Vitamins. Well so what?

B Vitamins have been proven to help your body breakdown carbohydrates and turn them into glucose, something your body uses for energy. If you are having problems digesting your food Vitamin B also helps breakdown fats and proteins.

You'll also notice several hair and skin products are fortified with Vitamin B. This super vitamin helps your cells work to regenerate themselves quicker and gives your skin a nice silky feel.

Depending on what you add to the kvass you can even get more of a "Health Drink". Beet Kvass is a popular drink that was (and still is used) throughout Europe to promote digestion, and cleanse the liver. Some people and take the occasional Kvass bath when they have the flu!

There are hundreds of mentions throughout the world that *Beet Kvass* is used for cancer treatment, liver cleansing, and infection control in the body.

These benefits may look familiar to you if you are a Kombucha fan. Kombucha is a fermented tea that is consumed in many Asian and Asian-Pacific countries.

While this isn't medically proven the drink was also used as a fertility agent. Many Europeans would give the bride Kvass on her wedding day to promote fertility.

Just drinking the Kvass is sometimes not enough. Often the spent grains or bread were fed to people and animals to help prevent the flu.

Yeast itself possesses some nice health benefits. From stress relief to sleeping easier, yeast is used for many at home remedies including cholesterol reduction.

In the summer months Honey was a popular addition to the refreshing beverage. Mead was quite popular so this was just another way to ferment the beverage and add sweetness. Remember, kvass has alcohol but wasn't an adult only drink. It was and still is served to children.

Since honey sugars are fermentable this raised the alcohol level and added more flavor.

Just SOME of the benefits of honey are: reducing your weight, providing energy with small amount of calories, improving digestion, antibacterial, antifungal, provides antioxidants, Vitamin C, and Calcium.

If you're looking for sweeter kvass I would highly recommend adding honey. If not for the flavor then for all the good stuff it provides!

In short this isn't your regular fermented beverage; it is actually very healthy.

What do I need to make Kvass?

You will easily find everything you need to make kvass in your kitchen. The equipment you have to have:

- *Boiling pot (at least 1 gallon)*
- *Fermentation vessel (can be as crude as a glass jar or you can have an airtight plastic "Brewing Bucket")*
- *Strainer*

Equipment you don't NEED but can come in handy

- *Hydrometer (used to measure Original and Final Gravity)*
- *Thermometer*
- *Cheese Cloth (to use in conjunction with your strainer)*
- *Bottles*
- *Bottle capper and caps*

We'll go into detail about how you will use all of this, but you won't NEED anything special to get your first batch started.

What ingredients will I need to start making Kvass and how do I use all this stuff?

There is a WIDE interpretation of what can go into Kvass. You will however need water, yeast, and some fermentable sugar.

First make sure your boiling pot is about 50% larger than the batch size you intend to make. If you are making a gallon on kvass, get at least a 1.50 gallon boiling pot. You are adding sugar to the water and it tends to boil over.

Your strainer can be the same one you use for your pasta, but if you are making kvass with a fruit that has a bunch of seeds (think strawberries) you may want cheesecloth for a finer straining. I would recommend cheesecloth for all kvass; it allows you to have a much clearer drink and provides a much easier cleanup.

Next is a fermentation vessel. If you have a sour palate let me recommend an open fermentation (one without a lid). Wild yeast and bacteria will likely jump into your fermentation and it gives you a taste anywhere from fruity to extreme sourness. While this will affect the consistency of your brews, it may lend to some unique flavor that you will fall in love with.

I like to open ferment just about all of my kvass. Sometimes there are huge variations in the flavor of the kvass even when the exact same ingredients are used.

I would try both open and closed fermentation, see what you like best and roll with it!

To do a closed fermentation you will need some type of brewing bucket. These can be found at homebrew stores or on the internet with ease. They range from $8-$20. These have airtight lids with a blow off tube.

THIS BLOW OFF IS THERE FOR A REASON! Don't think you can substitute a mason jar or some other device with a lid. The yeast will burp off CO_2 to the point that the container will explode! Be safe; get one with a blow off tube.

Now comes the Hydrometer. This instrument is a small blown glass weighted object that measures Original Gravity and Final Gravity of your brew.

Before you pitch your yeast take the Original Gravity reading. This tells you how much fermentable sugar you have to deal with. When the brew is done fermenting, take the Final Gravity reading.

What these numbers will tell you is how much alcohol you have in your drink. Some hydrometers have "potential alcohol" on the scale so you won't have to do any math or run to your computer to put in the numbers and get the alcohol reading.

This also helps you know when your kvass is done fermenting. Once you get a reading around 1.008 your beer is close to or done fermenting and ready for drinking/storage.

While this isn't completely necessary it helps you with consistency in your brews and also lets you know how much you can safely consume.

Something else you will need is sanitizing equipment. You will want to clean well all of your equipment before and after use. This will help your yeast act better and give you a better tasting beer.

Whatever you use make sure you rinse it well. A bleach tasting kvass is probably not that good for you...or tasty.

Another tip is to make some extra ice the night before. If you want to cool your wort (your strained kvass) quickly you can fill your sink with ice and water and drop your container of water into the mix for a speedy cooling.

Adding the Yeast

Homebrewers of beer and wine will know that pitching the yeast at the exact correct temperature is critical to your brew.

If you are using packets of bread yeast, add when the water is lukewarm (70 – 85 degrees Fahrenheit).

If you are using brewer's yeast (made specifically for beer) you will want to be closer to 70-75 degrees for proper fermentation.

Whatever yeast you use, please read the directions of when to add it.

Don't panic when adding the yeast...more than likely it will work.

Some rules of thumb though...if the water feels hot, cool it more. If it feels cooler than the room temperature, you may need to heat it up. Most yeast doesn't like to work in temperatures below 60 degrees.

The warmer your kvass the faster the ferment, the cooler, the slower. Either way....DONT PANIC!

How should I drink and store my Kvass?

In a word...FRESH! Since Kvass has such little alcohol inside, it will not keep for a very long time. If you don't bottle it and eliminate oxygen from reaching your drink you will drink a nice cool glass of vinegar within about 12 – 15 days.

Store your kvass in used beer bottles (buy a capper and caps to seal them), or in the fridge in a closed container (after fermentation). The cold temperature will slow the growth of any bacteria that will reach it.

From the first day your kvass is able to be consumed I would drink it all within a week for the best taste. It will last up to 3-4 weeks if stored in a sealed container. The taste will deteriorate (or enhance depending on your tastes), but after a month it is done. Sealing it off will also add some carbonation to the drink.

Some of my friends prefer the "flat" kvass while others really like the carbonated type. I would experiment with each and see what you like better. If you do not seal it off, the carbonation will just go into the air giving you "flat" kvass.

Another tip for drinking kvass is the lower the alcohol content, the quicker you should drink it.

Kvass Recipes

While you can follow all of these exactly feel free to experiment! They will be broken down by types of Kvass:

- *Bread Style Kvass – Real Bread Added*
- *Fruit Kvass – Fruit added.*
- *Herb/Mint Kvass*
- *Honey Kvass*

I believe this is the most kvass recipes in one source that you will find. There are 25 recipes in here, some very traditional, some absolutely NOT traditional.

That said you could generate another 250 if you wanted. Add your favorite fruit if it's not here, make your own bread then add it to the kvass, whatever you think will work please go for it. Use these recipes as a base for your inspiration.

I've actually made bread with kvass as the liquid, then added the kvass bread to the kvass! Think of it as recycling.

If you look around you may even find a few recipes that use rye or wheat flour as a substitute for bread. You won't find any of those recipes here. I find they are hard to deal with, messy, and don't provide a very nice flavor. It is also harder to strain and you end up with a much cloudier drink.

If you must try it, make sure you stir it very well if you are boiling the water. The flour sinks to the bottom and it tends to burn.

Kvass making should be fun and there is absolutely something in here that will excite your taste buds! Feel free to go off the beaten path an experiment with your own wizardry and invent your own Kvass!

If you think you have created something *really cool* email me the recipe at Dan@beaverbrewingcompany.com and we can see if we can include it into the next volume of this Kvass book! I'd like to double the recipes in the next volume.

Beaver Brewing Company Kvass

Let's start with the Beaver Brewing Company ™ Favorite! This is a semi-traditional Kvass. I have scaled this down to a 1.5 to 2 gallon batch.

Ingredients:

½ Loaf of Rye Bread
1 Loaf of Sourdough
1 Loaf of Pumpernickel
1.5 pounds of malted wheat or rye
1 to 2 Lemons
2 gallons of water
1 cup of raisins
1/8 cup of sugar
(optional) .5 ounces of Hersbrucker Hops
½ Vial of Brewer's Yeast or 2 packages of bread yeast

Process:

Slice the bread. Heat oven to 250 degrees Fahrenheit. Place the bread on a 2 – 3 cookie sheets, space them out so they can dry out.

Leave in the oven for 30 - 45 minutes or until they are dried out.

Heat 2.25 gallons of water in a pot to 170 degrees. Place all of the bread and wheat malt into a container, add the water. Cover and let sit for 1 hour.

Strain out the water. Restrain through cheesecloth to try and clarify your wort.

Add wort (what you just strained) to boiling pot. Bring to boil. (This is when you would add the hops if you were using them). Take off heat then cool your wort to 75 degrees then add to your fermentation vessel.

Add the juice from the lemons. Also add your raisins to the fermenter. Add yeast. Allow to ferment 3-5 days.

After Fermentation, add 1/8 cup of sugar that has been dissolved in water (preferably boiled then cooled) to the now fermented kvass. Put into bottles add cap off. Store at room temperature for 4-6 days. Put in fridge to cool then open and enjoy!

Optional: Add raisins to the fermenter or to the bottles for some extra flavor.

Bread Kvass Recipes

These are the most traditional kvass style recipes. Almost all old school recipes for kvass call for a loaf of bread. This is the base of your drink. Again, I can't stress this enough. Don't buy the cheapest bread out there for your kvass. If you like it and eat it all the time, please use that bread.

Rye Bread Kvass

This is a traditional Rye Bread Kvass. Great starter kvass if you have never brewed one before.

Ingredients:

1 Pound of Rye Bread (Approximately 1 Loaf)
.75 Gallon of water
4 ounces of Sugar
1 packet of dry yeast

Slice and dry bread in a 250 degree oven. Put water and dried bread into a pot. Bring water to 170 degrees, stir contents, cover and turn off heat. Let sit for 1-3 hours.

If the water has not cooled to room temperature put in the fridge until it reaches 70-80 degrees. Strain the water.

Add the yeast and the sugar to the water. This should start fermenting relatively quickly (within a few hours).

When you see a layer of bubbles or foam you can strain again (optional) and then pour into bottles.

Toss in a few raisins if you would like to each bottle. Leave at room temperature. Put in the fridge after 3-6 days then open and enjoy!

You can also drink the kvass even more fresh if you would like. Traditionally the kvass would be drank "flat" after fermentation was complete (6-24 hours). Try it both ways to see what you like best!

Sour Sourdough Kvass

Bread Kvass that will get a touch of sourness to it. If you like it EXTRA sour let out in the open for 2-3 full days to allow wild yeast to enter your concoction.

Ingredients:

2 Loaves of Sourdough Bread (1 if a large loaf)
1.5 Gallons of water
4 Ounces of Sugar
2 Lemons
1 Package of Dry Yeast

Cut and dry bread in a 225 degree oven. Bring water to 170 degrees, add the bread. Let sit for 1-3 hours. Strain the water out. Add the juice of your lemons.

If you would like some bite to your drink you can add the rinds to your fermentation. This will add a little bitterness to the drink.

Add yeast after the water has cooled to room temperature. To allow some wild yeast into your kvass DO NOT COVER or seal off your fermenter. Also, you can add a day or two to your fermentation. Best if you drink 1 or two days after fermentation.

You can also bottle and allow aging for 3-6 days if you would like some carbonation in the drink.

Petersburg Pumpernickel Golden Kvass

One of my personal favorites….Pumpernickel will give your kvass a slightly darker color, but don't think it will be black. Just a bit more copper. For this one I actually add golden raisins. We'll do something a little different to the raisins to get even more sugars and flavor out.

Ingredients:

1.5 Pounds of Pumpernickel (2 Loaves)
2 Cups of Golden Raisins
1 Gallon of water
½ Cup of Sugar
1 vial of brewer's yeast (optional)
You can also use the dry bread yeast

The night before you make this start your raisins…coarsely chop them or put in your food processer to make it easy on yourself. Add them to 4-5 cups of water and let sit for the night at room temperature.

Slice the bread and put into 250 degree oven until dried out.

Add bread and water to boil pot. Bring water to 170 degrees, add bread, ¼ cups of sugar, and your raisin mixture to the water and take off the heat. Let sit for 1-3 hours to cool. Strain and add your other ¼ cup of sugar and your yeast.

Let ferment, bottle and let age for 4-6 days. There is a touch more sugar in this one so let it age an additional day.

This is great Kvass to enjoy the day you make it.

Off the Wall Bread Recipes

Ok, I am sure a 10th century Russian would never have made one of these next few recipes, but these are actually pretty good. They are here to show you that you can really take your kvass anywhere you'd like.

Cinnamon Raisin Bread Kvass

Forgot about the Cinnamon Bread you had in the back of your freezer? Here is the perfect home for it. Great on a cool fall afternoon.

Ingredients:

1 pound of Cinnamon Raisin Bread
1 Cup of Raisins
2 Cups of Sugar
1 packet of yeast
Cinnamon Sticks (1-4 too taste)
1 gallon of water

Cut bread and place into 225 degree oven until lightly toasted. Add bread, water, and sugar to boiling pot. Raise to 150 degrees then take off heat, uncover, let sit for 1-3 hours until cooled.

Add yeast and let ferment for 12-24 hours. Strain again.

You can bottle this, but I would just toss in the fridge and drink as soon as it cools for a great fresh drink. I have even heated it up a bit and added more cinnamon sticks for a nice warm drink!

For intense cinnamon add sticks at the boil. For a more subtle flavor add to your fermentation.

This is great to share at Thanksgiving with the whole family. The Aroma is amazing. Also a great starter for Pumpkin Soup!

Fruitcake Kvass

So your Aunt Vera gave you ANOTHER fruitcake this Christmas that you know no one in your family will consider throwing away until March. A great way to use that paperweight is in Kvass. Tons of flavors and sugars are in that fruitcake and you will have a VERY cool Christmas drink this holiday. If you want to kick it up this holiday season add a shot of rum to your glass!

Ingredients:

As much fruitcake as your aunt makes (1 – 2 loaves)
1 Cinnamon Stick (Optional)
Dried Fruit Mix (Optional)
½ cup sugar
1 Gallon of Water
2 yeast packets
Rum (Optional)

Chop up the fruitcake very thin. Put in 250 degree oven until dried. Fruitcake has plenty of moisture in it so this may take longer than your regular bread. Less water is needed because this bread dosen't soak in so much of the moisture.

Add water, ½ of the sugar and fruitcake to pot and raise to 160 degrees. This is where you can add more diced dried fruit / cinnamon sticks. Let cool for 1-3 hours. Stain well. There will be a lot of sediment in this one...trust me.

Add the rest of the sugar and yeast to the wort to ferment. Bottle and let age for 3-5 days. Cool in the fridge overnight and enjoy. Don't add the rum during the ferment. The alcohol in the rum could slow down or stop your fermentation.

I would put a damp cloth over the fermentation of the kvass or use a brewing bucket with a blowoff. This is one you don't want wild sour east getting into.

Glazed Donut Kvass

I told you this book had some less than traditional recipes in it!

Just like when cooking with wine, don't go cheap. If you wouldn't drink it, you shouldn't cook with it...if you wouldn't eat it...don't kvass with it. (Just used kvass as a verb, a literary first as far as I am concerned!)

Find your favorite glazed donut and prepare for a sugary treat! Great to bottle and let carbonate, tastes like a yeasty energy drink!

12 Glazed Donuts (or whatever your favorite donut is)
1.5 Gallons of water
1 Cup of Golden Raisins
1.5 gallons of water
2 packets of yeast

Dice your donut and spread them over a few cookie trays. Place in the oven at 225 degrees. These will get gooey from the glaze melting off a bit in the oven...pour as much as you can into your boil pot. Add the water and raisins then raise to 160 degrees. Take off heat and let cool for 1-3 hours.

Add your yeast and let ferment for 6-7 hours until you see a nice foam on top. Either bottle or cool down in the fridge and enjoy. This is a sugary dream if you are into sweet drinks.

Now the tricky part is there will be some oil in this from the butter/fat from the donuts. Whenever you see this floating at the top, try and remove it. When it cools it will rise to the top, this is another good time to take it out.

Cuban Kvass

While Kvass isn't a Cuban drink by any means (unless the communists brought it over during the cold war years), Cuban Bread makes a GREAT Kvass bread. It is about 3 feet long, has a hard crust but plenty of airy insides that suck up a bunch of water.

Think of a very large French baguette...that's what this is.

You can also kick it up with some traditional Cuban spices in the fermenter like Cilantro, Peppers, Tumeric, or Garlic if you are making a soup stock!

1 Loaf of Cuban Bread
1 Gallon of water
1 packet of yeast
1 Lemon Peel
Spices (optional)

Chop up bread into 2 x 2 inch pieces. This is airy and soaks up a bunch, this will make it easier to extract the water. Put in 250 degree oven and move them around every 15 minutes so they don't burn.

Put water and bread into boil pot, raise to 170 degrees then let cool for 1-3 hours. Strain WELL, maybe even twice. This bread breaks apart quite a bit.

Add yeast and any spices you would like. Great starter for Kvass soup. Let ferment for 6-24 hours, enjoy cool.

Greek Kvass (salad dressing)

I didn't find one mention of Greek kvass in all of my research but honest to God this makes one of the best starters for a Greek salad dressing. Crazy, I know. But give this a try it you want a tangy dressing for your next dinner party. Pita's ad some body to the dressing.

Ingredients:

2 Lemons
¼ Cup of Sugar
4 Pitas
3 tablespoons of fresh Thyme
1 Tablespoon of Oregano
4 Cups of Water
1 Cup of Olive Oil
¼ cup of red wine vinegar
1 packet of yeast

Place your pitas in the toaster. After toasted chop into quarters. Mix pitas, sugar, lemon juice, spices and water into your boil pot. Bring to 140 degrees. Take off heat.

When room temperature, strain then add your yeast and open ferment overnight. Put in a dressing container(s). Add your Oil and Vinegar and shake the hell out of it to emulsify. If you want to kick it up add some feta cheese crumbles!

FRUIT & VEGETABLE KVASS RECIPES

As stated before Kvass was actually a "health drink" back in the day and people were always adding more healthy items to the Kvass. Fruit was a natural choice since it contained sugar, sweetness, and flavor.

Probably the most traditional Russian Kvass that is used for health benefits if the Beet Kvass.

So what's so damn special about Beet Kvass? Here is a list of everything Beet Kvass is and has been used for:

- A Digestive aid
- Cleansing of the Liver
- Reduction of the size of kidney stones
- Treatment for Irritable Bowel Syndrome
- Cancer treatment
- Blood detoxifying

Here are some other things in beets: Tons of Vitamin C which is good for your immune system....Rich source of Folates that help the DNA in your cells....Plenty of Glycine Betaine, this removes toxins from your blood...and did I mention a Beet only contains about 50 calories? It also has some fiber in it for good measure.

In short it is a wonder root. I have included 4 separate recipes for the Beet Kvass itself since it is probably the most popular kvass behind bread kvass.

The process of making them is different and they all are unique in their own way. People have even been known to bathe in it!

TIP: Wear gloves when cutting up your beets...if not you will have "bloody" looking hands!

Beet Kvass #1

This is the earthiest tasting kvass of the bunch. The salt brings out the flavor of the beet and covers up some of the bitterness the root provides.

If you only want the health aspects of the drink and no alcohol you can eliminate the yeast. However the yeast does add tons of flavor and the small amount of alcohol can actually be good for you!

Ingredients:

2 Large Beets
2.5 Quarts of distilled water
1 Tablespoon of Himalayan Sea Salt
1 Lime (Optional)
1 Package of Yeast
3 Tablespoons of Sugar

Wash and peel beets. Chop finely to extract the most sugar you can from the beets. In a large jar(s) add your water, sugar, yeast and beets. You do not have to boil the water.

This is an instance where you may want to use a yeast starter (instructions at the beginning of the book).

Let ferment for 24 hours. Enjoy fresh (recommended) or add another 2 tablespoons of sugar and bottle.

If you are enjoying fresh add the sea salt, it adds a nice kick and brings out the earthy flavor.

Beet Kvass #2

This is a little more of a sour Lactobacillus taste to it. Still provides a punch of flavor.

Ingredients:

2 Large Beets
1 Tablespoon of Sea Salt
2 Beet "greens"
3 quarts of water
¼ Cup of Goat Whey or regular whey

If you want more lactic acid cut in 1 inch cubes. If you want more alcohol flavor shred the beets. Lactic Acid helps digestion so if that is your goal go for it.

Warm water to 150 degrees. Add water, beets, salt, fermenter or a jar, let cool then add your whey. Let sit for 24 hours then enjoy!

Beet Kvass #3 – Beet Pop (or soda depending on where you live)

This will be a carbonated beverage which some people just have to have. We will also be fermenting this so alcohol will be present. Myself, I prefer the first two, but this is also tasty and looks beautiful in a glass tumbler.

2 – 3 Large Beets
1 Cup of dried Cranberries (optional)
2.5 quarts of water
1 dry yeast packet
¼ cup of sugar

Wash, clean, and shred your beets.

Bring water to 100 degrees (optional). Add all contents except yeast into your fermenter. Add the water. Let cool overnight. Strain and add yeast and another tablespoon of sugar. Let ferment for 1-3 days or until foam from the top goes away.

Bottle and let carbonate for 5 days. Cool in your fridge then enjoy! You may want to take hydrometer readings on this one since we are adding some more sugar to the mix and shredding the beets. I have done this and got up to 2.1% ABV and you may not want it that high.

Looks like a red sparkling wine when pouring from the bottle.

Beet Kvass Earth Blend

Want a very rich, earthy, and powerful taste that is packed with a crazy amount of healthy stuff? Try this version. Many use this as the base for salad dressing. It is best consumed in small 3 oz quantities when you wake up and after dinner.

Ingredients:

2 Large Beets
2 Cloves of Garlic
2 Tablespoons of caraway seeds
2 quarts of water
1 Tablespoon of Himalayan Sea Salt
1 Teaspoon of Crushed Black Pepper

Clean beets and chop into 1 inch cubes. Place all the ingredients including the water into a jar. Close and let sit for 24 hours. Strain VERY well. Chill in the refrigerator and enjoy.

For the salad dressing add 1 cup of olive oil, and ¼ cup of your favorite vinegar (mine is tarragon), and shake the hell out of it before serving.

The Lithuania Lemon

A personal favorite of mine, I really love lemony kvass and I go overboard on this one. If you want more of a bitterness to the drink, ferment the beverage with the lemon rinds.

This is one I would recommend a brewer's yeast. Preferably a California / IPA style yeast. This will really make the lemon pop and give you some great carbonation to your beverage.

Ingredients:

4 Large Lemons
3 quarts of water
1 Loaf of Oat Grain Bread
½ Cup of sugar
California/IPA Brewing yeast

Squeeze the juice from the lemons and put aside. Bring the water to 150 degrees and add the bread that you have sliced and dried out in a 225 degree oven. Also add ½ cup of sugar.

Let sit for 2-3 hours until cool. Add the lemon juice to the mixture. Strain well with cheese cloth.

Add yeast and let ferment for 3-5 days. You can open or close ferment this beverage. I prefer closed so you get a nice lemony taste. Add another 3 tablespoons of sugar then bottle. Wait another 4-5 days then enjoy!

BrewBerry Kvass

This is more of a "beer" than kvass but it is worth the extra work. You'll need some malted wheat which adds a unique sweet backbone to the drink. The blueberries will give you drink an awesome color and a freshness that will allow you to drink this all in one day.

This is kvass you will want to use a hydrometer on to measure the alcohol. I'd also recommend a thermometer.

Ingredients:

1 Pound of Blueberries (Preferably fresh)
1.5 Pounds of Malted and Crushed Wheat
1 Loaf of Multi-Grain Bread
1.5 Gallons of water
2 cups of green tea
½ cup of sugar
½ cup of blueberry honey (optional)
.5 ounces of yeast

Heat water to 165 degrees then add your malted wheat and dried out bread. Put the wheat in a fine mesh bag so you can easily take it out and strain it. Let the wheat sit for 45 minutes.

While heating your water put blueberries, honey, and sugar in your blender. Add the tea to make it come together and puree…

Remove the grain bag. Add the puree and bring to boil. DO NOT BOIL YOUR GRAINS! This will give you a very astringent flavor (think of biting into a coffee filter).

Take off heat and cool. Add yeast and let sit till the foam starts going away. When it is done or close to done fermenting, cool off in your fridge and drink it that day. A nice sweetness if you add the honey and the wheat brings it altogether.

You can bottle, but it is awesome fresh.

Ginger Tea Kvass

This provides an INTENSE Ginger flavor and gives off a very nice aroma. I made this without the tea and to be honest it is overpowering, at least for me. I think the green tea balances it out well. Also makes a great "stock" if you are making chicken stir fry.

1 Fresh Ginger Root
2 Quarts of Brewed Green Tea
¼ Cup of Sugar
1 Lemon
1 yeast packet

Brew the tea. Shred your ginger root (not too much, this stuff is strong!). While tea is still warm, put your ginger, sugar, and lemon juice in. Let sit until it cools to room temperature.

Add yeast and open ferment. The wild yeast will pair well with the ginger flavor. Will ferment for about 1 day.

Bottle for a carbonated "ginger pop" or drink fresh.

Cinnamon Apple Kvass

Perfect for a brisk cool day. I would highly recommend fermenting this one in a closed fermenter, or at least put a moist cloth over your jar.

3 Apples (pick your favorite)
2 quarts of water
2 sticks of cinnamon
½ cup of maple syrup
¼ cup of sugar
1 package of yeast

Boil water, add apples (chopped into small pieces), cinnamon sticks and syrup or sugar. Take off heat and let cool. Add your yeast and prepare for a fast ferment.

I don't know the science behind it, but when I work with apples they seem to ferment in under a day. Cool after fermentation and consume fresh with a Thanksgiving Turkey!

Whey Your Raspberries

If you want more probiotics whey is the way to go. This is what is in your yogurt and what makes that so good for your digestive tract. We will use it here because it will give you a nice sourness that pairs well with the raspberries.

Since making kvass should be fun and some people HATE measuring stuff we will make this as easy as possible...hopefully.

Ingredients:

Raspberries
2 oz. of whey for every quart of water
Water
Glass jar

Get your largest glass jar you have, fill up your jar ¼ full with fresh raspberries. Get a wooden spoon and break them up a bit. Add your whey...fill the rest of the jar with lukewarm water.   Stir...

Let it work itself out for about 36 hours at room temperature then toss in your fridge.

Strain and drink cold!   Provides a clean sour taste that is backed up by the tart raspberries.

Pomegranate Kvass

The tartness of the Pomegranate Juice pairs nicely with the sourness of some lemons and open fermentation. The juice is also packed with anti-oxidants and other goodies that make it a great natural healer.

I like adding some pumpernickel bread to give the drink some body and added flavor.

Ingredients:

2 Cups of Pomegranate Juice
½ loaf of Pumpernickel Bread
2 Quarts of water
1 yeast packet
1-2 lemons (optional)

Bring your water to a 130 degrees and add your juice, and bread (add lemons if you want). Take off heat and wait until it cools to around 80 degrees. Strain well into your fermenter.

Add your yeast and when you see a thick froth toss in the fridge for 24 hours. Take out and enjoy.

Mint Kvass

For a person that grows 5 types of mint (yes there are differences in mint) in their backyard I was very excited to find out that mint was a staple in early kvass.

You may not think of mint as a healthy item but there are some that think that mint slows or maybe stops the growth of several types of cancer. This is because mint contains the phytonutrient perilly alcohol.

It has also been linked to helping with Irritable Bowel Syndrome.

You will usually find mint in tea, but this is an excellent addition to any homemade kvass. Plus the aroma makes you smile even before you drink it.

Mint makes your kvass pop, it adds such a fresh flavor to it you can't help yourself but to have 2 or 3 glasses at a time.

I'm not going to offer many mint only recipes because it is easy enough to add the mint when you have the craving for it. Here are two mint Kvass drinks that I particularly enjoy.

MinTea

So mint and tea go together...why not add bread?

Ingredients:
1 Loaf of Rye Bread
4-5 sprigs of Pineapple Mint (or any mint)
2 quarts of water
1 tablespoon of sugar
1 packet of yeast

Cut up bread, place in 225 degree oven until crisp. Add water, sugar and bread into your boil pot and raise to 160 degrees. Allow to cool and then add your yeast when you place into your fermenter. Strain well.

This is when you want to add your mint. If you cook it the mint can give off a bitter astringent flavor. Open ferment for 1-2 days.

This is one I would bottle. Tastes great and refreshing when some carbonation is added.

Lemomintade Kvass

Something about mint and lemon together...if you could put the taste of sitting on you back porch at sunset into a drink it would absolutely have mint and lemon together.

Ingredients:

4 Lemons
4-5 sprigs of curly mint (or substitute)
3 quarts of water
¼ cup of sugar
½ loaf of pumpernickel bread
1 package of yeast

Dry your bread in the oven and juice your lemons. Boil your water and add your ingredients other than the yeast and mint. Bring to 140 degrees then cool down. Strain well.

After cool, add your mint and yeast. When frothy toss in the fridge. After it has cooled you can drink 'til your heart's content!

Honey Kvass

If you got the need for mead than this is your drink. Mead is one of the earliest fermented drinks and kvass is a lighter alcohol version of mead. Honey is another wonder food that provides dozens of healthy additives to your cool drink.

Honey mead is much higher in alcohol than kvass and is made more like wine than kvass. Worth taking original and final gravity reading with these recipes, they can get to over 3% ABV.

Honey & Lemon Raisin Kvass

Sweet and smooth. Comes out very clear since no bread is involved. You still need to strain though since the honey comb doesn't completely break down.

Ingredients:
1 Honey Comb
1 Cup of Raisins
2.5 quarts of water
1 Lemon
1 Package of yeast

Dissolve honey in hot water (no need to boil but you can). Add the raisins and lemon juice and allow the water to cool to lukewarm. Add your yeast. Once it is frothy put something over the container, maybe a wet cloth and let ferment overnight.

Strain well then put into bottles. Wait 2 days than pop in the fridge overnight.   It will last for about 2 weeks in the bottle.

Sweetbread Honey Kvass

If you have never bumped into sweetbread you are missing out. This is traditional Portuguese bread made with the addition of sugar and sometimes dried fruits. It is usually light and floury so it absorbs tons of water.

Some of the breads include a "mixed peel" which have candied fruit peels throughout the bread, if you can find that I would highly recommend using that.

½ Cup of clover honey
3 quarts of water
1 loaf of sweetbread
1 package of yeast
½ cup of dried cranberries (if no fruit in the bread)

Slice bread and place into 225 degree oven until crispy. Bring water to 150 degrees and dissolve the honey in the water and add your bread.   Let sit until lukewarm. Add your yeast and let ferment for 24-36 hours. Strain well then place in your refrigerator and when cooled pour into a glass and enjoy the sweetness.

Honey Fig Kvass

My personal favorite among the honey kvass recipes.
The key is the figs, if you can find fresh please use
those. Dry Figs provide a deep brown color to your
drink and if you bottle it the pour will look like a nice
American Amber Lager.

Ingredients:

8 ounces of dried figs
1 honeycomb
2 quarts of water
½ loaf of rye bread (optional)
1 package of yeast (or use a hefewiezen brewer's yeast
for a banana like finish)

Put figs into blender with 1 cup of water. Make a paste.
Dry your bread if you are adding. Put bread,
honeycomb, and fig puree into your boil pot. Raise heat
and stir until honey is dissolved (make sure to stir, this
one can burn since the figs go to the bottom.

Take off heat and cool to lukewarm temperature. Add
your yeast and ferment for 36 hours at room
temperature. STRAIN TWICE! Tons of little seeds in
those figs of yours.

Place in bottles and let age for 3 days. Move to your
fridge to cool then pop these out with a few friends, it
will go quickly!

Tips for making your kvass...

Sometimes it just gets lost in the sauce. You read the whole book but you overlooked these items.

When Dealing with Bread Kvass...

Always strain well and try letting the "trub" (aka muck at the bottom of your fermenter or boil pot) stay right where it is. You will have a much prettier (and tastier) drink in the end.

Don't use starch white bread. Unless you're eating a turkey sandwich there is really no reason to ever use this type of bread. It is tasteless and doesn't offer much in terms of nutrition compared to grainy breads.

Make sure you dry the bread. If not it will get very glue like and make a mess. Plus you won't extract as much flavor out of it.

When Making Fruit Kvass...

If you are using dried fruit, hydrate it well.

Don't boil herbs or fruits for long periods, and sometimes not at all. They can become very bitter if overcooked.

When Making Honey Kvass

Always make sure the honey is dissolved completely.

Strain out the wax from the honeycomb.

Make sure you stir when boiling, the honey takes awhile to dissolve and can burn on the bottom of your pot if you don't.

When Using Herbs

Almost any herb or fruit rind will get very bitter if you cook it too long. To eliminate that bitterness don't add until after you are done boiling the wort. The leafier the herd the more bitter it will get under extreme heat.

How do I know my yeast is working?

You will see a frothy top on your wort and it will be bubbling away if you are using a blow off top.

How do I know the yeast is done working?

No bubbles in your blow off tube or you will see that the frothiness is gone and the drink looks clear. Also check your hydrometer readings.

Really, My Kids can drink this?

I am the LAST person to tell someone how to rule their own home, but I can say that in Europe Kvass is shared with everyone in the family that has reached an age that they can drink from a glass.

Acknowledgements

Thanks to my wife for trying all the kvass I ever make even though she "hates" beer. If she can get it down I know I have done well.

Also thanks to my parents and my sister that constantly are telling people that they need to try kvass and they know where you can get it.

A special thanks to my cat Bemus who continuously walked across the keyboard during the writing of this book and made it more of an adventure than it had to be. If there are any typos I balem thmm on hm.

And a Special Thanks to you for buying this book. Thank you is something we have gotten away from in the last few years but I GREATLY APRECIATE IT! Even though you have already helped me please do one more thing for me...more for yourself but I am asking...

Make Kvass with a friend or family member. It may taste nothing like you would like but the experience alone will be worth it...trust me.

And as always, email me at dan@beaverbrewingcompany.com. I actually read and respond to just about every email I get.

And Finally...THANK YOU AGAIN!

Kvass Notes:

Kvass Name:

Date Brewed:

Ingredients I used:

_____

_____

_____

_____

_____

Process:

_____

_____

_____

_____

Tasting Notes:

Next Time I make I will change:

Kvass Notes:

Kvass Name:

Date Brewed:

Ingredients I used:

_____

_____

_____

_____

_____

Process:

_____

_____

_____

_____

Tasting Notes:

Next Time I make I will change:

34239115R00040

Made in the USA
Charleston, SC
03 October 2014